ADULT COLORING BOOKS

THE OCEAN

BEACH COLORING BOOK
For Adults

SHINE BOOKS

San Diego, California

Seashells are love letters in the sand.

Seas the day.

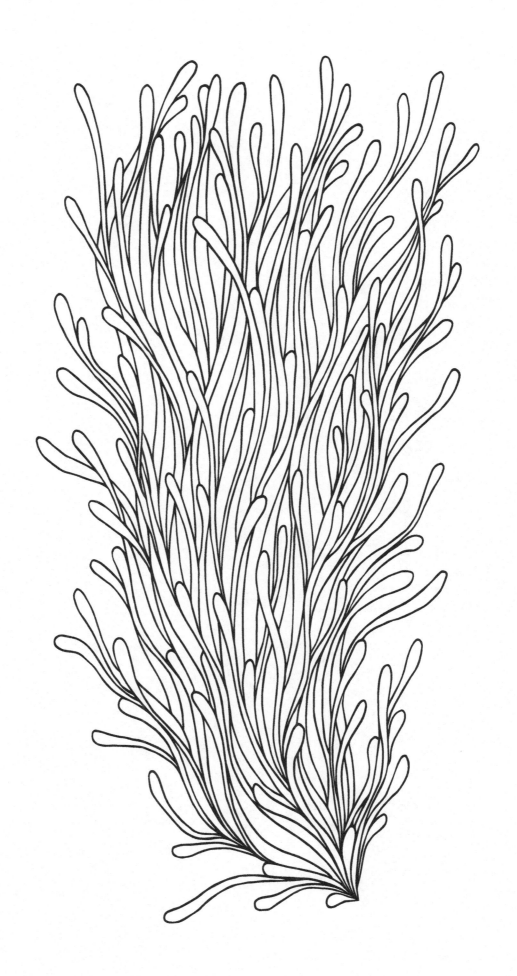

I'm happy anywhere I can see the ocean.

let the sea
set you free

The voice of the sea sings to the soul.

The ocean is where I belong.

Dream higher than the sky
&
deeper than the ocean.

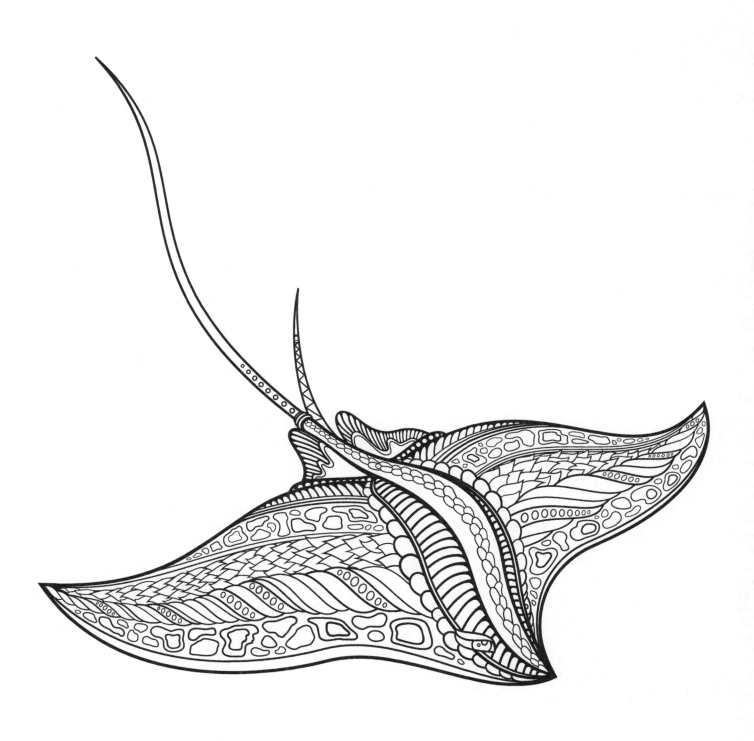

may you always have a shell in your
pocket and sand in your shoes.

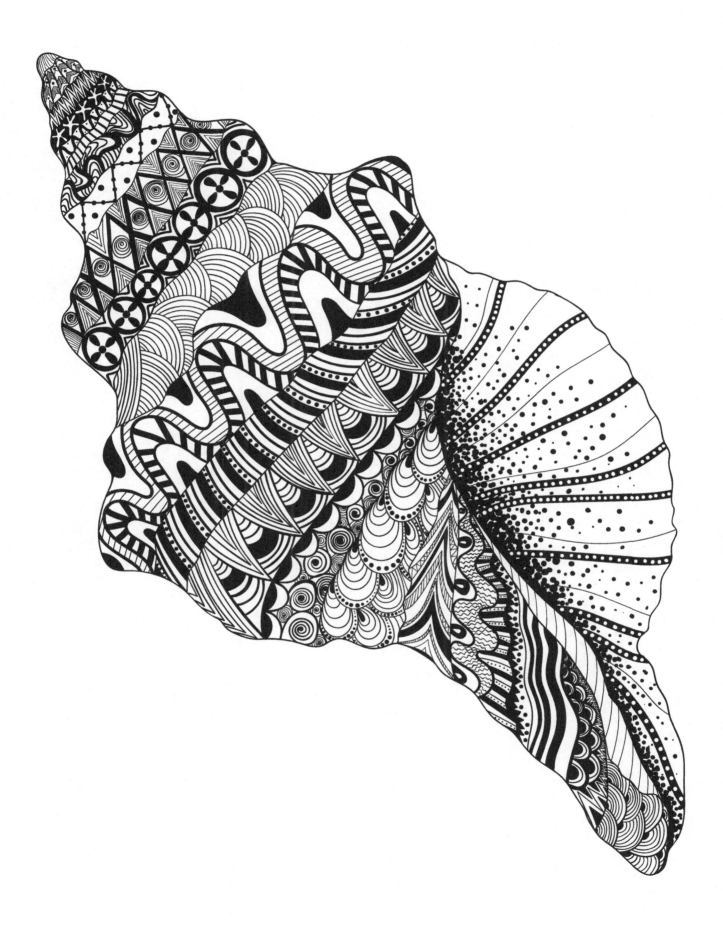

I can leave the sea,
but the sea never leaves me.

TAKE me to the SEA

Every little thing's gonna beach alright.

The sea is the place for me!

The sea makes me feel like me.

Be like the dolphin.

Sandy toes and salty kisses.

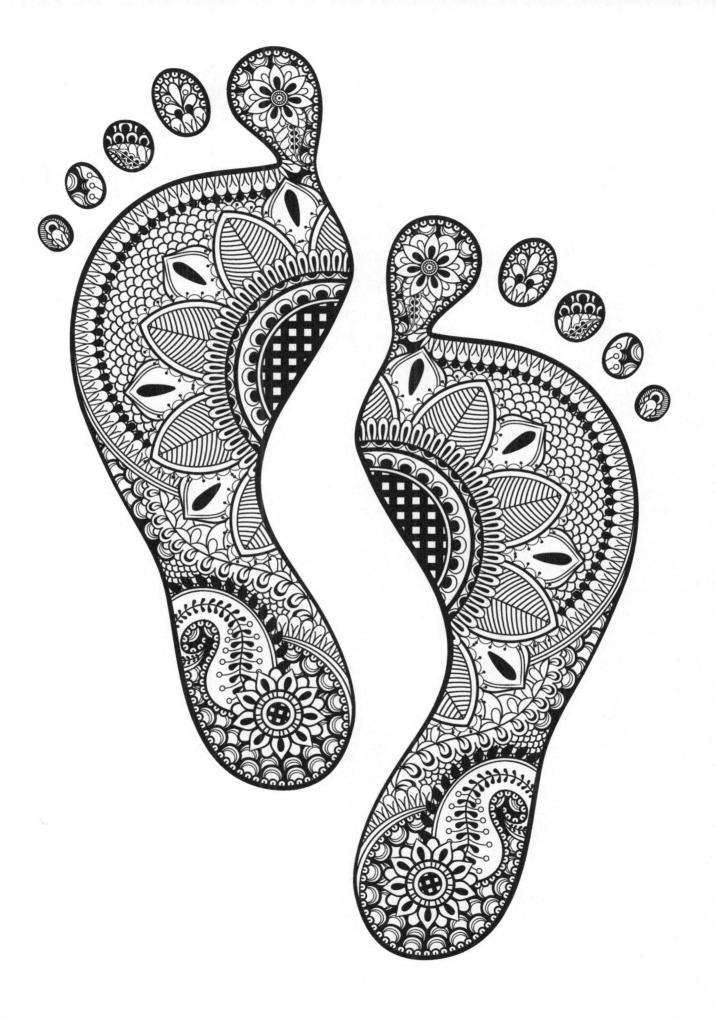

Dive in!

The sun touches my soul.

A smile can change the world.

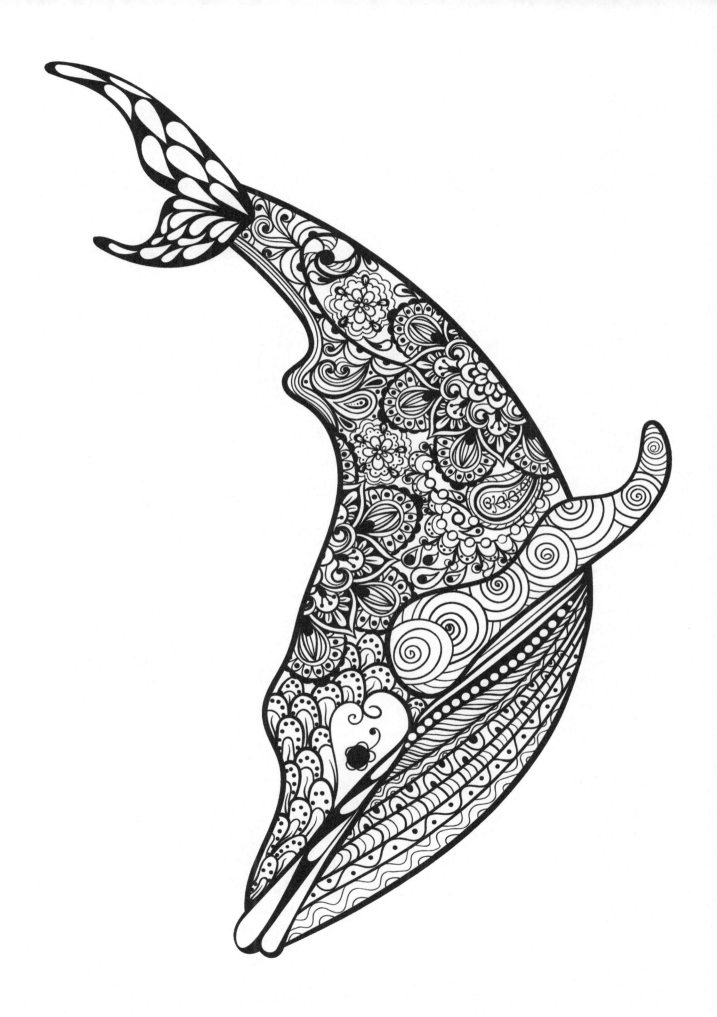

A day at the beach restores the soul.

Dreams are made of sand and sun.

Dear ocean,
Thank you for making me feel tiny,
humble, inspired, and salty all at once.

All you need is a good dose of
vitamin sea.

when life gives you lemons, squeeze one
in your hair and go surf.

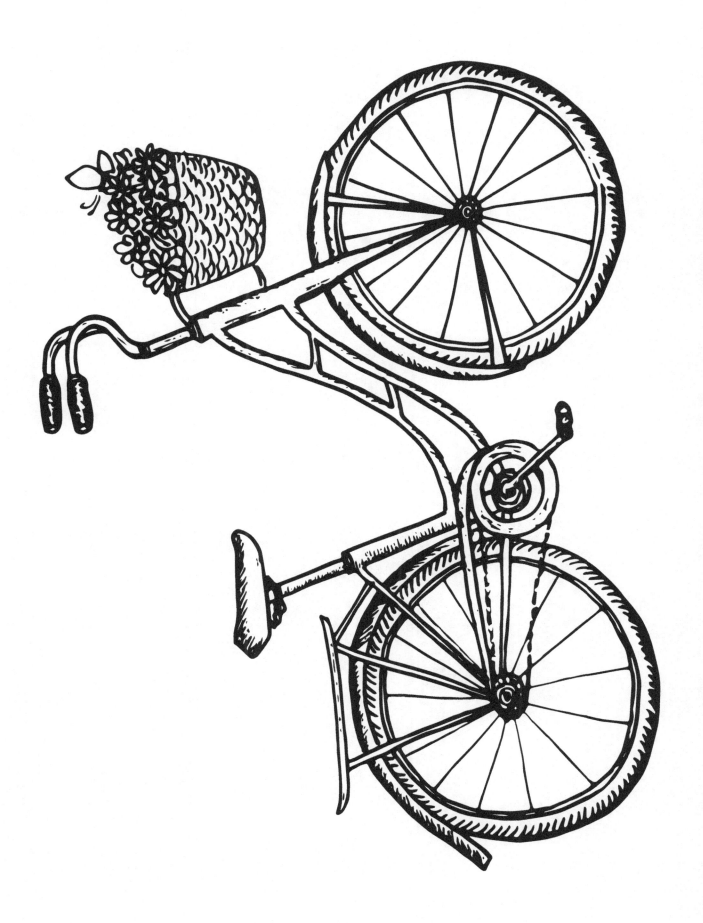

I choose to go with the flow.

There's no place like home,
except the beach.

Not all stars belong to the sky.

The waves of the sea
bring me back to me.

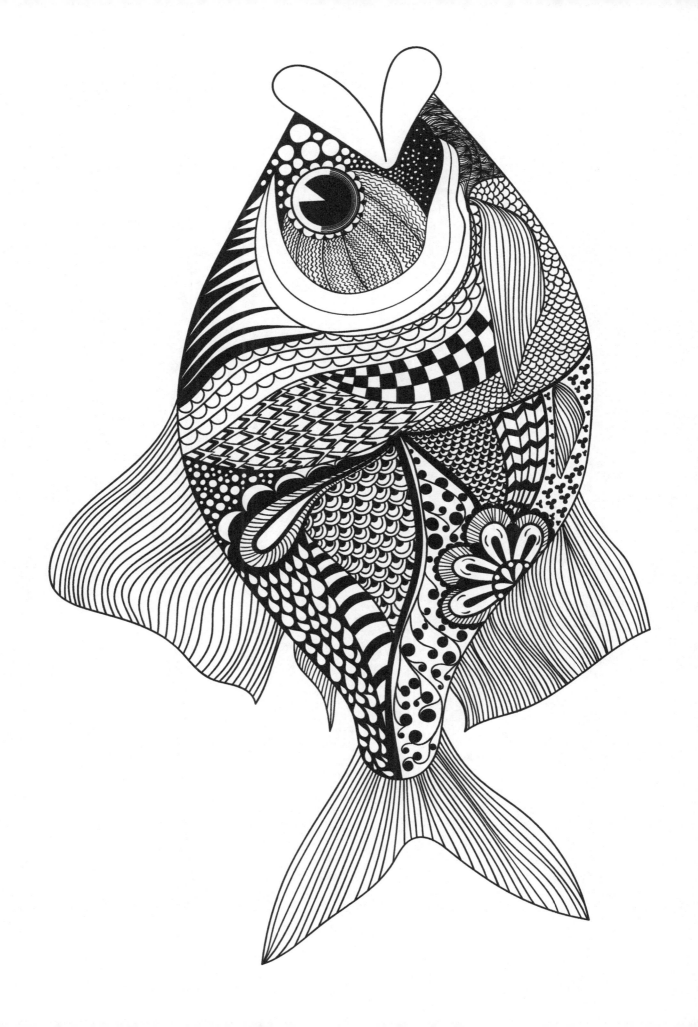

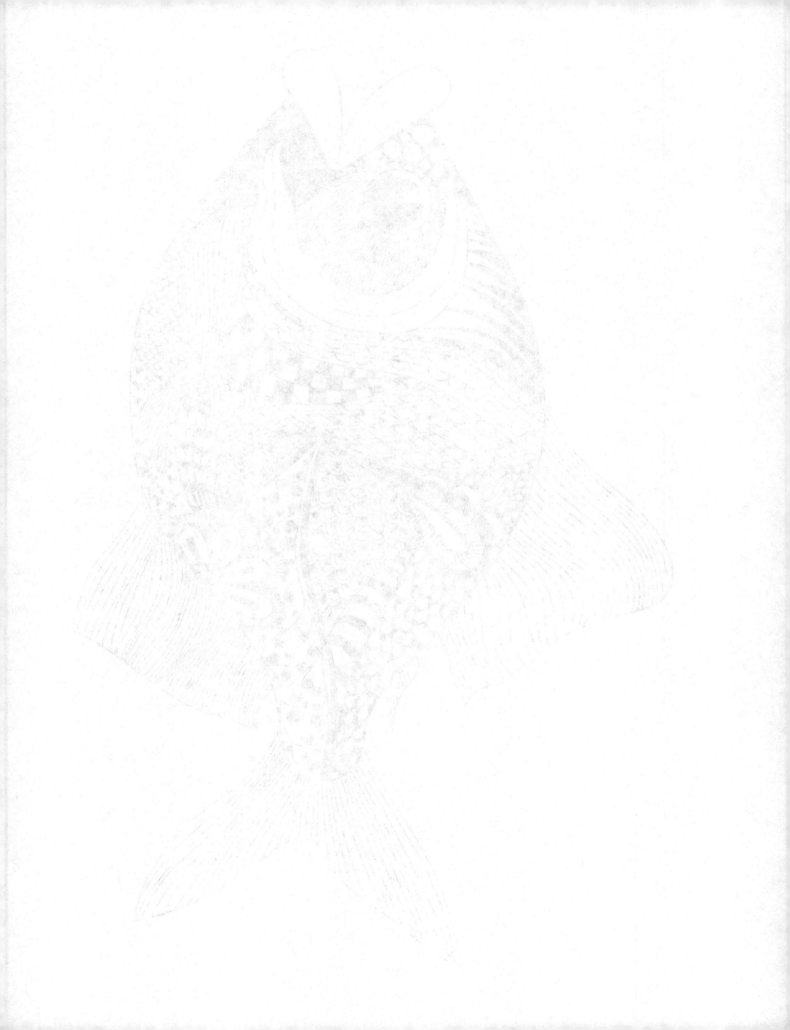

Relax, unwind,
get in a flip flop state of mind.

I am wild, beautiful and free,

just like the sea.

Where there's a will, there's a wave.

Let the currents guide your heart.

The sea, once it casts its spell, holds one in its net of wonder forever.

~Jacques Cousteau

Now is the perfect time to relax...

The ocean is calling

Write your worries on the sand
and
watch them wash away.

Happiness comes in salty water.

Smell the sea and feel the sky.
Let your soul and spirit fly.

~Van Morrison

I'm happy anywhere I can see the ocean.

Cherish every sunset.

Gone surfing.

Summer lovin'.

Wrinkles will only go
where smiles have been.

~Jimmy Buffet

Palm trees, ocean breeze.

Peace
Love
Ocean
Waves

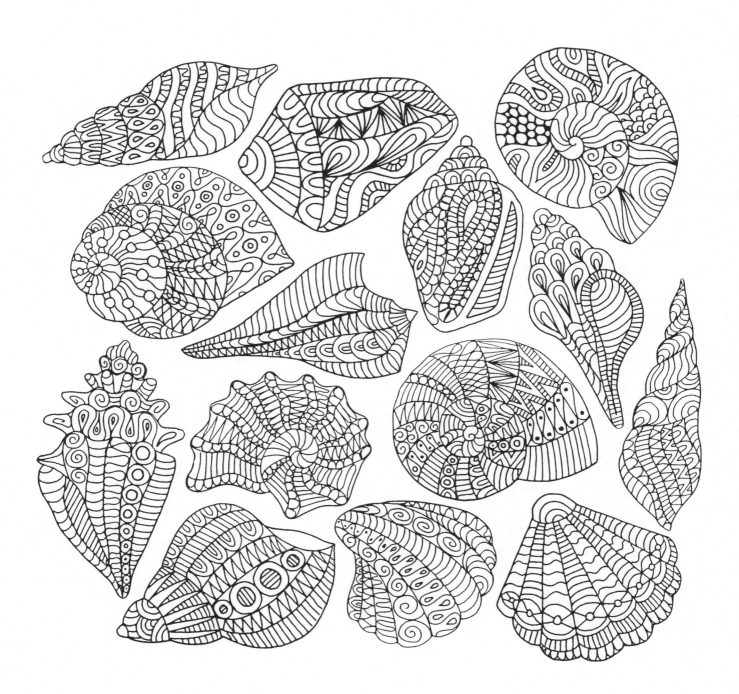

FOR MORE COLORING FUN FROM  , CHECK OUT

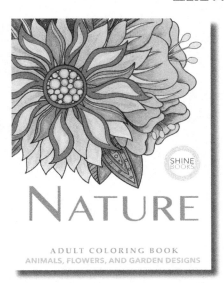

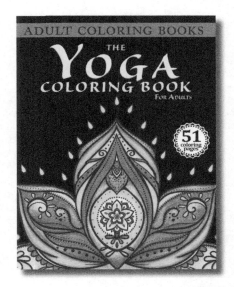

STAY UPDATED ON NEW TITLES, FIND OUT ABOUT GIVEAWAYS, AND FOLLOW US AT:

 #ShineAdultColoringBooks

 ShineAdultColoringBooks.com